Middle World 1947

Animal Camouflage

Animal
Camouflage

Janet McDonnell

THE CHILD'S WORLD®, INC.

Library of Congress Cataloging-in-Publication Data
McDonnell, Janet, 1962-
Animal Camouflage/by Janet McDonnell.
p.   cm.
Includes index.
Summary: Describes forms, methods, and purposes of camouflage as
used by different members of the animal kingdom.
ISBN 1-56766-400-8 (alk. paper)
1. Camouflage (Biology)—Juvenile literature.
[1. Camouflage (Biology)] I. Title.
QL767.M35   1997
591.47'2—dc21   96-30079
CIP
AC

Photo Credits

COMSTOCK/COMSTOCK, Inc.: 20
COMSTOCK/Art Gingert: cover
COMSTOCK/Denver Bryan: 19
COMSTOCK/Gwen Fidler: 9
COMSTOCK/Franklin Viola: 29
DPA/DEMBINSKY PHOTO ASSOC: 24
Fritz Polking/DEMBINSKY PHOTO ASSOC: 13
Gijsbert van Frankenhuyzen/DEMBINSKY PHOTO ASSOC: 2
Jim Roetzel/DEMBINSKY PHOTO ASSOC: 23
Larry Mishkar/DEMBINSKY PHOTO ASSOC: 15
Rod Planck/DEMBINSKY PHOTO ASSOC: 16
Skip Moody/DEMBINSKY PHOTO ASSOC: 26, 30
Robert and Linda Mitchell: 6, 10

On the cover...

Front cover: A *polar bear* sits in the snow.
Page 2: The *great horned owl's* feathers look like tree bark.

Table of Contents

Have you ever played hide and seek outside? Sometimes it is hard to find a good place to hide! But what if you could paint yourself brown and green like the ground? Or put on a costume that made you look like a tree? Or lie down and cover yourself with leaves? All of these tricks would make you much harder to find.

A forest looks green and brown.

What is Camouflage?

Some animals use tricks to hide themselves. Using colors and patterns to hide is called **camouflage**. Camouflage makes things very hard to find—even when they are out in the open. Animals, fish, reptiles, and even people use camouflage for hiding. When something looks like the objects around it, it is much harder to see. That is what camouflage is all about!

A *walkingstick* looks like the branches around it.

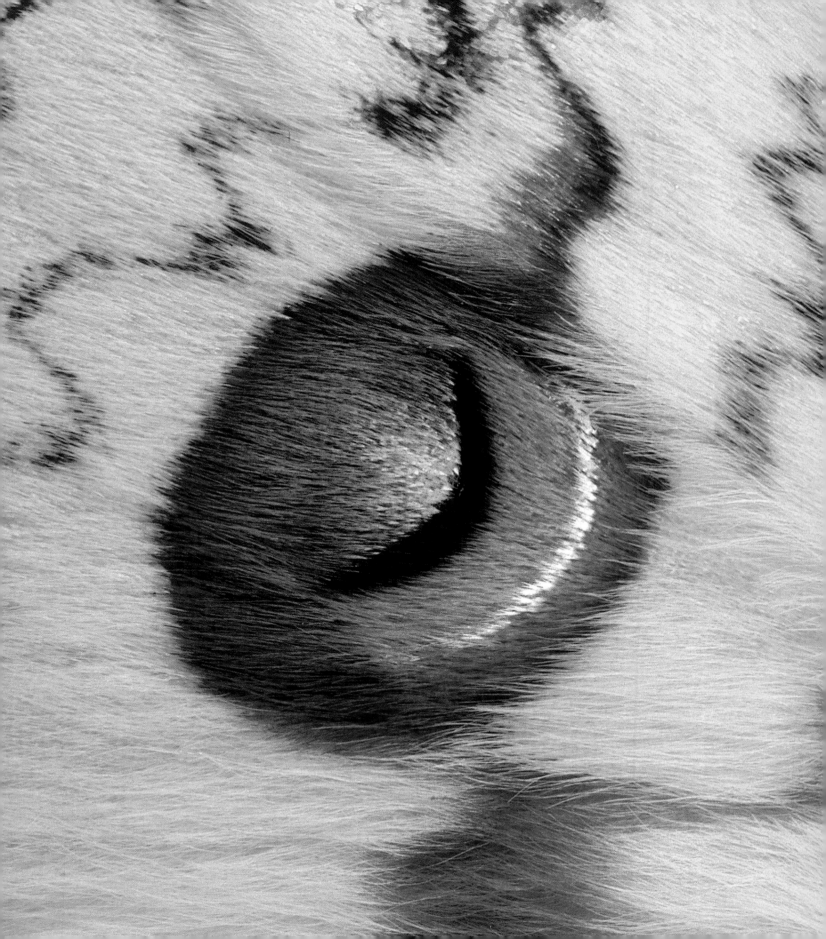

Why Do Animals Need Camouflage?

There are many reasons why animals hide. They often hide from their enemies. Some animals move around at night and sleep during the day. They need to stay hidden while they sleep. Other animals hide so that they can be better hunters. Camouflage helps them sneak up on their dinner.

This *emperor moth* has an eyespot on its wing to scare enemies.

How Do Animals Use Camouflage?

Animals use camouflage in many different ways. Some use it to blend in with the objects around them. These objects are called **surroundings**. The *polar bear's* white coat blends in with it's surroundings—the white snow. This color hides the bear when it is hunting for seals. The *black bear's* dark coat helps it hide in dark trees and bushes.

The white fur of this *polar bear* looks like the snow around it.

But what happens if an animal's surroundings are more than one color? Some animals have camouflage with more than one color, too! Some fish have dark backs and white bellies. When a hungry bird looks into the dark water, the fish's dark back is hard to see. But to an enemy deeper in the water, the fish's white belly blends in with the bright sky.

This *large mouth bass* has a dark back that matches the water.

Why Do Some Animals Change Color?

Sometimes an animal's surroundings change. Then the animal has to change color, too! That is the only way it can stay hidden. Some animals change color to match the season. The *snowshoe rabbit* changes color very slowly in the spring and fall.

This *showshoe rabbit* has white fur to match the snow.

In the winter, the snowshoe rabbit's fur is white like the snow. As the snow melts in the spring, the rabbit grows patches of brown fur. It looks just like patches of ground and melting snow. Then summer comes, and the ground is brown. The rabbit's fur grows brown to match. When fall comes, the rabbit starts to turn white again.

This baby snowshoe rabbit has brown fur in the spring.

Do All Animals Use Colors to Hide?

Some animals use designs, or **patterns**, instead of changing colors. Blending into a pattern is a good way to hide. When an animal's body looks like its surroundings, it is very hard to find.

A **fawn**, or baby deer, is too weak to run fast. But it can hide by lying still. The fawn's back is covered with dots. The dots look like spots of sunlight on the forest floor. If the fawn stays still, it is very hard to see.

Fawns like this one can blend into their surroundings.

Another animal that uses patterns to hide is the *bittern*. This bird lives in marshes with tall grass. The stripes on its feathers look just like shadows in the grass. When the bittern is in danger, it makes itself even harder to find. It points its beak straight up and sways its body in the breeze. The bittern looks just like the blowing grass!

This bittern has patterns that match the tall grass.

What Is Mimicry?

Some animals have a shape or color that looks like something else. This type of camouflage is called **mimicry**. Animals that use mimicry are good pretenders.

The walkingstick is one insect that uses mimicry. Its long, thin, bumpy body looks just like a small branch! Walkingsticks can even change color with the seasons. In the spring, the tree's branches and leaves are green. The walkingstick is green, too. When the branches and leaves turn brown, the walkingstick turns brown to match.

This walkingstick looks like a branch.

Some animals use other kinds of mimicry to fool their enemies. Some moths have large spots on their rear wings. The spots look just like eyes! When the moth is resting, its front wings cover the spots. But when the moth senses danger, it lifts its front wings and shows the spots. If an enemy is afraid of the big "eyes," it will leave the moth alone.

The spots on this *Io moth's* wings look like eyes.

Some animals even make their own costumes for camouflage. The *masked crab* uses seaweed to make a costume. First the crab uses its claws to tear the seaweed into pieces. Then it puts each piece in its mouth and chews it until it is soft. The crab sticks the pieces of seaweed to itself. Little hooks on its shell and legs hold the seaweed in place.

This masked crab has used many things to make its costume.

From a rabbit that changes color to a crab in a seaweed costume, there are many kinds of camouflage. But each kind of camouflage has the same important job—to help animals hide. Now that you know some of their tricks, maybe you will see animals where you never saw them before. But you'll have to look very carefully, or you might be fooled!

This *zale moth* is hard to see because it looks like the tree trunk.

Glossary

camouflage (KAM-oo-flazh)
Camouflage is hiding by using colors or patterns. Animals use camouflage to blend in with their surroundings.

fawn (FAHN)
A fawn is a baby deer. The spots on a fawn's back look like sunlight on the forest floor.

mimicry (MI-mi-kree)
Mimicry is a kind of camouflage. When something uses mimicry, it makes itself look like something else. Walkingsticks use mimicry to look like little branches.

patterns (PA–turnz)
Patterns are designs. Many animals have patterns on their bodies that help them hide from enemies.

surroundings (suh ROWN–dingz)
An animal's surroundings are the objects around it. Many animals use camouflage to blend in with their surroundings.

Index

12/97